Decorative Origami
Boxes

Rick Beech

Illustrated by
Rikki Donachie

DOVER PUBLICATIONS, INC.
Mineola, New York

Planet Friendly Publishing
✔ Made in the United States
✔ Printed on Recycled Paper
Text: 50%   Cover: 10%
Learn more: www.greenedition.org

GREEN EDITION

At Dover Publications we're committed to producing books in an earth-friendly manner and to helping our customers make greener choices.

Manufacturing books in the United States ensures compliance with strict environmental laws and eliminates the need for international freight shipping, a major contributor to global air pollution.

And printing on recycled paper helps minimize our consumption of trees, water and fossil fuels. The text of *Decorative Origami Boxes* was printed on paper made with 50% post-consumer waste, and the cover was printed on paper made with 10% post-consumer waste. According to Environmental Defense's Paper Calculator, by using this innovative paper instead of conventional papers, we achieved the following environmental benefits:

Trees Saved: 18 • **Air Emissions Eliminated: 1,680 pounds**
Water Saved: 8,089 gallons • **Solid Waste Eliminated: 491 pounds**

For more information on our environmental practices, please visit us online at www.doverpublications.com/green

Copyright

Bibliographical Note

Decorative Origami Boxes is a new work, first published by Dover Publications, Inc., in 2007.

Library of Congress Cataloging-in-Publication Data

Beech, Rick.
    Decorative origami boxes / Rick Beech; illustrated by Rikki Donachie.
        p. cm.
    ISBN-13: 978-0-486-46173-1 (pbk.)
    ISBN-10: 0-486-46173-4 (pbk.)
    1. Origami. 2. Box craft. I. Title.

TT870.B4155 2007
736'.982—dc22

                                                           2007022355

Manufactured in the United States by Courier Corporation
46173403
www.doverpublications.com

Contents

Introduction

This selection of elegant origami boxes, including some designs previously unpublished, will delight both the beginner and the expert enthusiast. We recommend attempting the easier models at the beginning of the book first.

Rikki Donachie's beautifully-crafted and artistic diagrams will enable the reader to competently fold many differently shaped boxes and containers from one or several sheets of paper (this branch of origami is called "modular" or "unit" folding).

By way of a few tips, always fold carefully and accurately, and remember the "look ahead" rule of checking the next diagram to see that you have completed a particular stage correctly.

Never allow yourself to become impatient or frustrated with your first results; try the design again and again until you are totally delighted with the outcome. Origami is to be enjoyed!

Paper Choices

It is important when folding origami boxes to choose paper which is strong and sturdy, and which holds a crease well. The ideal stock to use is 80–100 gsm (grams per square meter), especially if the particular design is to fulfil a practical purpose; you may be making a confetti container for a wedding or a candy holder for a party, for example.

There are many sources for such material, including art suppliers, specialist gift shops and craft markets. You will notice on the covers of this book that for the best results highly coloured and patterned paper is recommended. Be creative!

Some instructions refer to A-size paper. This is an international paper size standard that uses the metric system. Some commonly used sizes are: A4 (8.27" x 11.69"), A5 (5.83" x 8.27"), and A6 (4.13" x 5.83"). These sizes are based on a single aspect ratio of the square root of two. The proportions of A-size paper always remain the same. For example: when an A1 size paper is folded in half, it becomes the size of an A2, when an A2 is folded in half, it becomes an A3, etc.

If you wish your box to be very sturdy and long lasting it is a good idea to glue flaps down and then to apply 2 or 3 coats of polyurethane varnish. Try the varnish on a scrap of the paper first as colours may run.

Creating Boxes

After folding all of the boxes in this book you may be tempted to create your own designs. It is easier than you might expect. Just by changing a valley to a mountain can have a dramatic effect if done in the right place. Keep experimenting with different shapes and maybe more than one piece of paper. Have fun!

When you have created a new design it is always a good idea to diagram it. This is also easier than you might expect. Rikki Donachie has, on his Web site, simple step-by-step instructions on how to draw origami diagrams.

Just visit; ***www.itsjustabitofpaper.com***

Guide to Symbols

—————————————————— Edge of paper or edge of fold

– – – – – – – – – – – – – – – Valley Fold

–··–··–··–··–··–··–··–··– Mountain Fold

———————————————— Previously made crease

······························· X-ray line of a significant edge

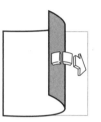

Lay paper white side up.

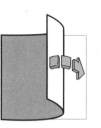

Lay paper white side down.

Unfold the indicated flap (check next step for result).

Fold in this direction.

Fold and Unfold.

Collapse on the indicated creases.

Revolve paper in the indicated direction.

Turn the paper over.

After completing this step, the model will not lie flat.

Repeat step on other side of paper.

The next step is enlarged for clarity.

 Hold the paper here.

Distance between 2 points.

3

Dividing an edge into thirds

For many origami designs we need to divide an edge accurately into thirds. The following method is convenient and accurate enough for most instances. With a bit of practice you will soon be able to do it very easily.

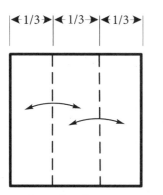

This is what the diagram might look like. Do not fold anything yet.

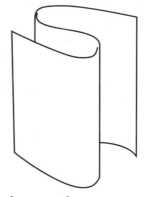

This is what you do...
Gently curve the paper into an "S" shape.
We will concentrate on the top edge for the next step.

Roll the paper until the edges line up with the curves.

Pinch   Pinch

When the edges are lined up with the folds pinch at the edges.

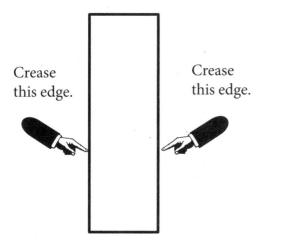

Crease this edge.   Crease this edge.

Lay the paper down flat and crease carefully and firmly along both edges.

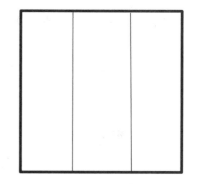

When you open up the paper, it should look like this.

This simple box can be made from rectangles of virtually any proportions. Often mistakenly called a printer's hat, it was actually used by printers to hold samples of ink.

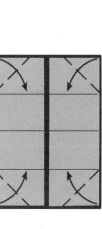

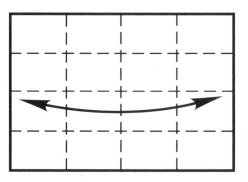

1. Crease into quarters both horizontally and vertically.

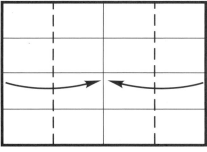

2. Fold the sides into the middle.

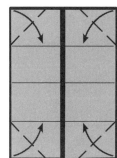

3. Valley fold the corners to the crease lines.

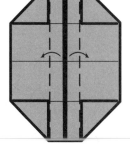

4. Fold the edges out over the top of the corners.

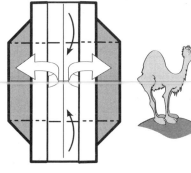

5. Open the box up while bringing the top and bottom sides in.

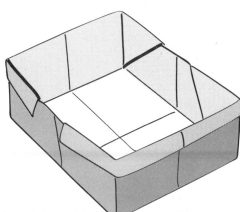

6. Pull the sides up.

7. The finished box.

Nik-Nak Box

Traditional

This is a very simple box that can be made from any "A" proportioned rectangle or a standard US letter size.

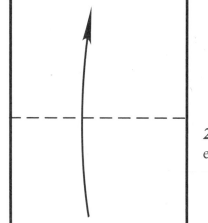

1. Lay the paper vertically.

2. Valley fold bottom edge up to top edge.

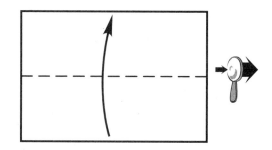

3. Valley fold in half upwards again.

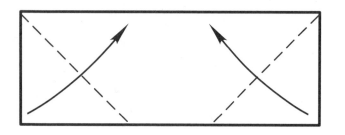

4. Fold the lower corners upwards at 45°.

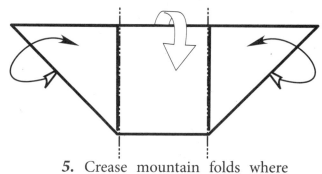

5. Crease mountain folds where shown and open out back to step 2.

6

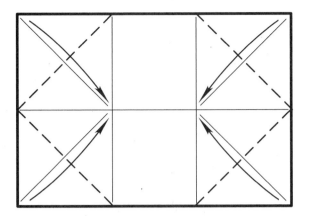

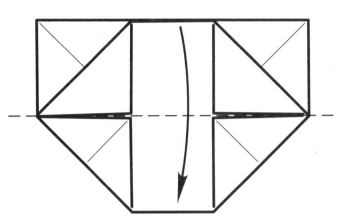

6. Fold lower corners up and a single layer of the top corners down, both at 45°.

7. Fold single layer down.

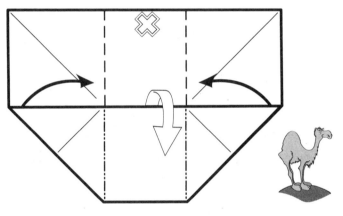

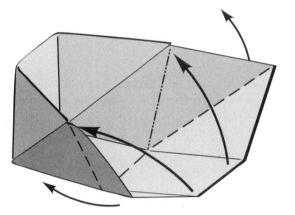

8. Open up the pocket while bringing the sides in. Note the valley and mountain folds. This will form a 3-D tray.

9. Bring the flat edge up while bringing the corners together on the outside.

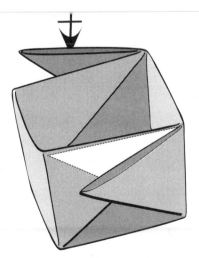

10. Tuck the sticky-out corners into the triangular pockets on both sides.

11. The finished Nik-Nak box.

Shallow Box
by Ted Normington

This simple box has a nice colour change effect using both sides of the paper.

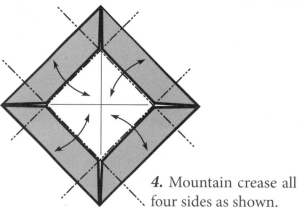

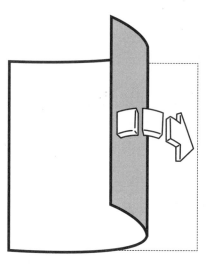

1. Begin with a square with the desired inside colour down.

2. After creasing the square in half in both directions, fold the corners into the centre.

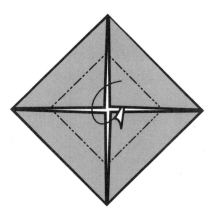

3. Mountain fold the corners under as shown.

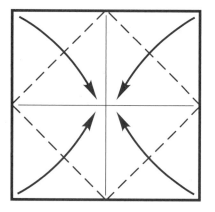

4. Mountain crease all four sides as shown.

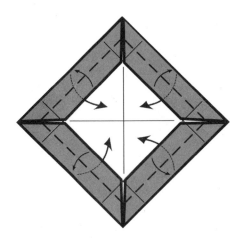

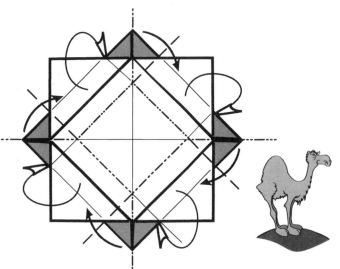

5. Fold the sides in half as shown, allowing the corners to open up completely, see next picture.

6. Collapse the box into shape using the previously made mountain creases. This view is of the base of the box.

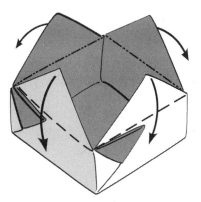

7. The collapsed box. Fold the large triangles down over the small triangles at each side.

8. Tuck the tips of the triangles under to lock the sides together.

9. The finished box.

Box in One

by Robert Harbin

This charming one piece box was designed by Robert Harbin, professional magician and one of the leading lights in origami in Britain in the 1960's.

Like many boxes it uses precreasing to form a final collapse.

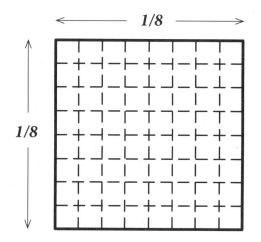

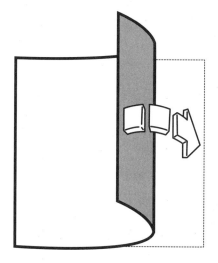

1. Begin with a square, white side up.

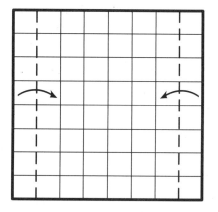

2. Divide the square into 8 equal divisions, horizontally and vertically.

3. Valley fold the left-hand and right-hand edges in on the creases.

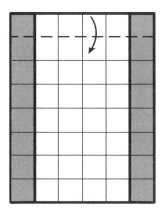

4. Valley fold the top down on the crease.

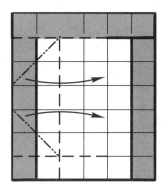 

5. Make the mountain creases shown and collapse the left side in using the creases.

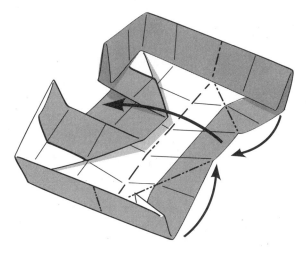

6. Repeat step 5 on the right-hand side.

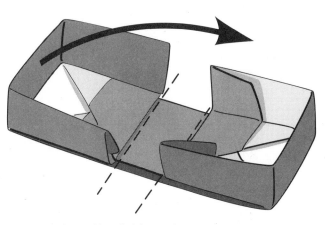

7. Make valley folds in the hinge to close the box.

8. The finished box.

A4 Thin Box
by Akira Nakamura

Begin with a sheet of A4 paper, or trim 12.5mm off the long edge of a standard US Letter (8¼″ x 11″) to obtain a rectangle of the same proportions (1 x √2).

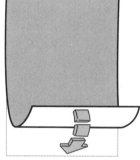

1. Lay paper white side down.

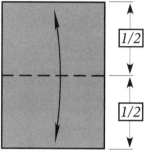

2. Crease in half.

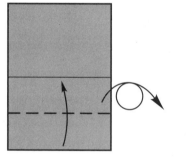

3. Fold bottom edge to halfway crease and turn over.

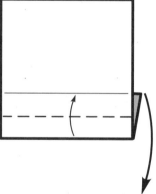

4. Fold bottom edge up to middle crease while allowing back flap to swing down.

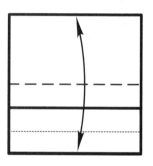

5. Bring top edge down to bottom edge to form a crease as shown.

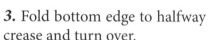

6. Valley fold the bottom edge up.

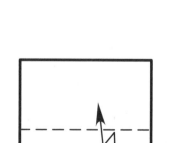

7. Zig-zag fold the bottom up.

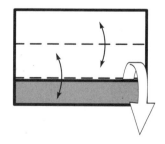

8. Crease the valley fold as shown and open out the entire sheet of paper.

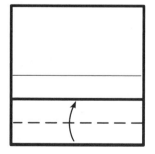

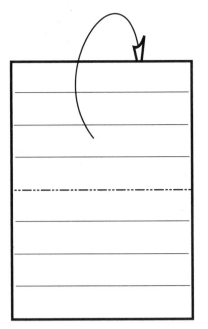

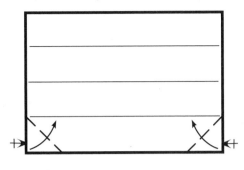

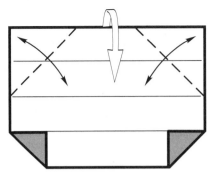

9. Mountain fold in half.

10. Fold corners up and repeat behind.

11. Crease top corners as shown and the open out. See next step.

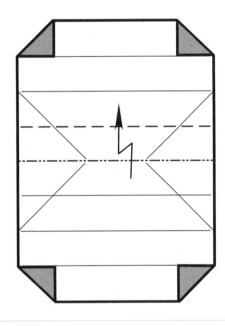

12. Zig-zag fold the middle upwards.

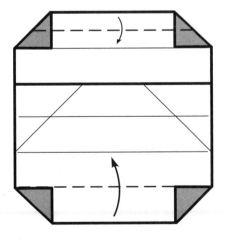

13. Valley fold as shown.

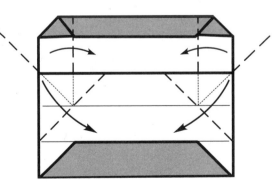

14. Fold the corners in and down along the creases made in step 11 and at the same time bring the sides in.

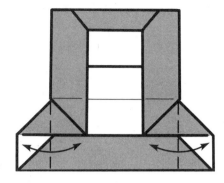

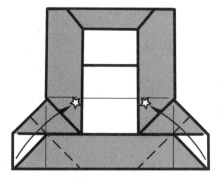

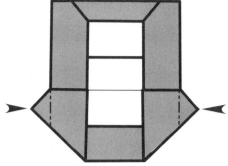

15. Crease the side flaps as shown.

16. Fold the bottom corners up as indicated. The corners will be tucked into the pockets beneath them in step 18.

17. Sink the two side corners in.

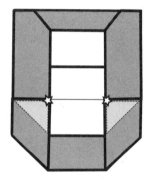

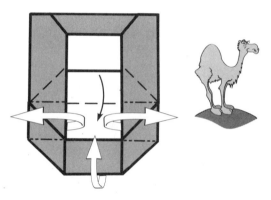

18. Tuck the corners marked with a star into the pockets beneath.

19. Open up the box on the indicated creases, bringing the lid towards you at the same time.

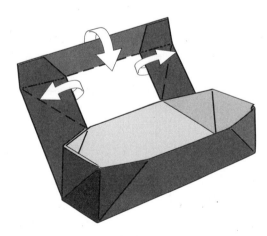

20. Open up the sides of the lid and shape it.

21. The finished box.

This is a traditional design from Japan. It is easy to make and, if you use fairly thick and brightly patterned paper, will produce a beautiful and sturdy box. Begin with 3 identical squares of paper.

Making the base:

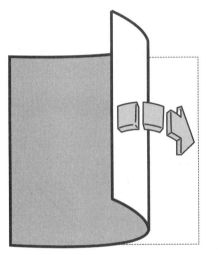

1. Start with a square of paper and lay it white side down.

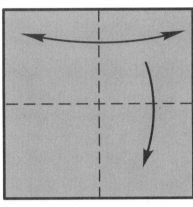

2. Valley fold and unfold in half vertically.
Note double headed arrow.
Valley fold in half downwards.
Note single headed arrow.

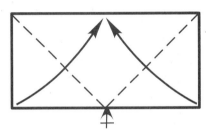

3. Valley fold corners up to the top edge.
Repeat behind, note the small arrow with the cross bar.

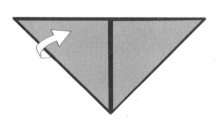

4. Open out. Look to the next step to see what it should look like.

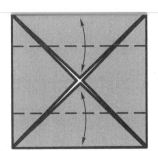

5. Note the double headed arrows.
A square that has all 4 corners folded into the centre like this is known as a blintz.

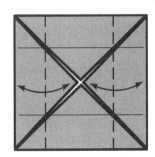

6. Fold and unfold the sides into the middle.

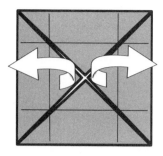

7. Open out the left and right sides.

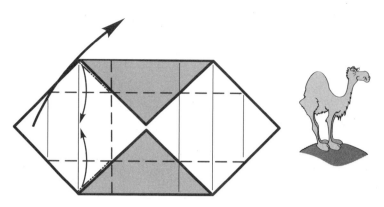

8. Look carefully at the creases and make the valley and mountain folds as shown, the left-hand corner will swing up towards you.

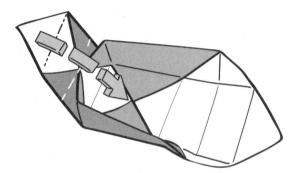

9. It should look like this! Fold the left-hand corner down into the centre.

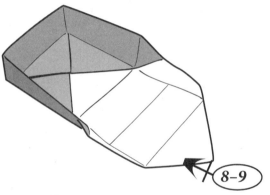

10. Repeat steps 8 and 9 on the right-hand corner.

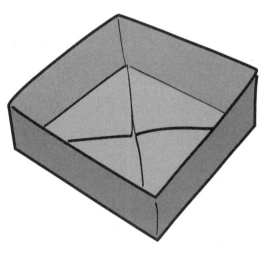

11. The completed base. Next we make a lid to fit.....

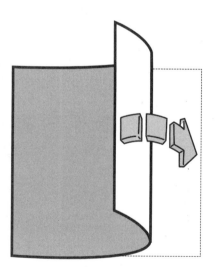

12. Take another square exactly the same size as the first square. Repeat steps 1–4.

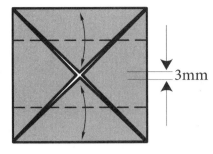

13. When you fold the top and bottom edges in leave a gap of approx 3mm between them.

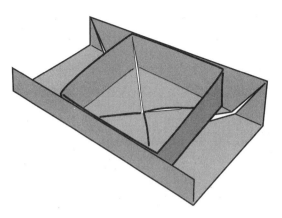

14. Check that the lid is a snug fit by fitting the box inside.

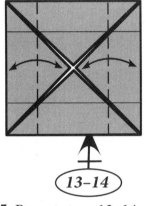

13–14

15. Repeat steps 13–14.

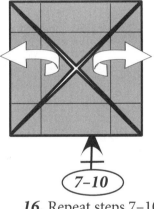

7–10

16. Repeat steps 7–10.

17. The base and lid are complete. Now for the internal divider...

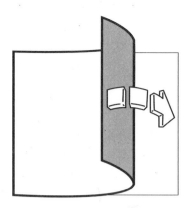

18. If you wish the divider to be the reverse colour of the box and lid, begin with the box colour down.

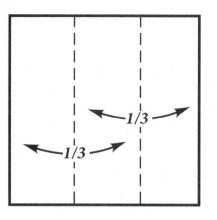

19. Divide the paper into thirds vertically (see page 4)...

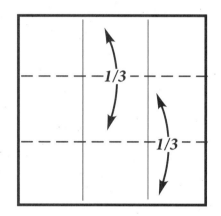

20. ...and thirds horizontally

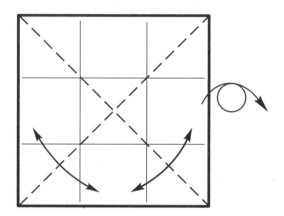

21. Valley fold on both diagonals. Turn paper over.

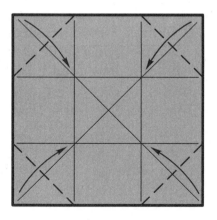

22. Valley fold all four corners to touch the outer corners of the central square.

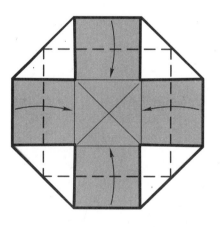

23. Valley fold the raw edges in to touch the outer edges of the central square.

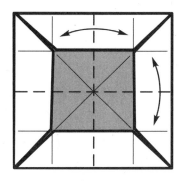

24. Valley fold as indicated.

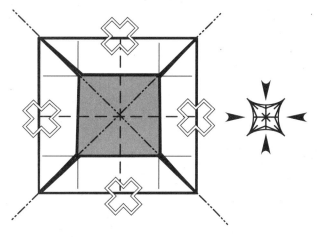

25. Hold the paper at the ✖ symbols and push your fingers together.
The symbol on the right means *"Collapse on the indicated creases"*.

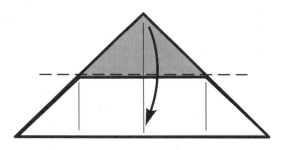

26. Valley fold the top point down.

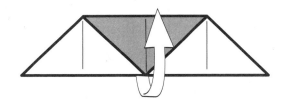

27. Take hold of the lower edge along with the small triangle and open out the 2 outer sections.

28. There is a crease running across the paper. Mountain fold in half using this crease. Place the divider flat on a table and press down firmly.

29. The divider is now ready to insert into the base.

30. The finished box.

Flower Box

by Fumio Inoue

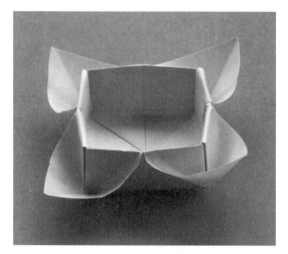

This pretty box is a simple variation of the Masu Box on page 15. Choose a paper in pastel shades to accentuate the floral effect.

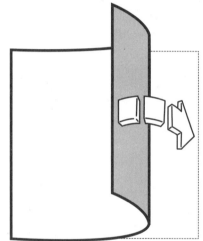

1. Begin with a square, white side up.

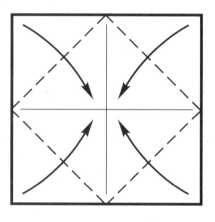

2. Fold the corners into the middle. This is known as a *"Blintz Fold"*.

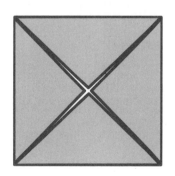

3. Repeat steps 2–8 of the Masu Box, pages 15-16.

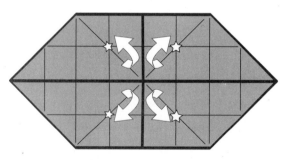

4. Lift up the corners from the stars. Do not crease, allow them to curve gently.

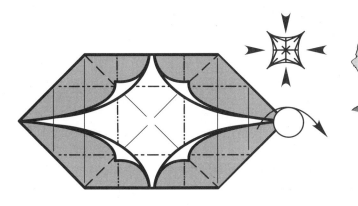

5. This view is of the base of the box. Collapse the box on the indicated creases, allowing the lifted corners to swing around to the front.

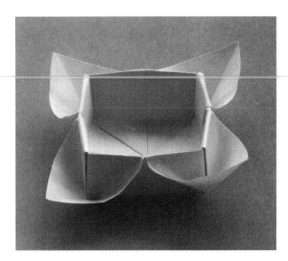

6. The collapse, viewed from the bottom.

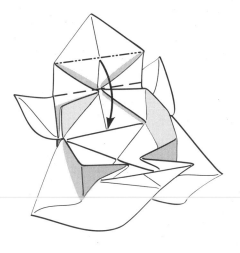

7. The top view.
Fold the flaps into the base as in the Masu Box steps 9–10.

8. The finished box.

Fancy Box with Ribbon

by Akiko Yamanashi

A delightful one piece box with an interesting contrasting ribbon detail. Choose paper that has different colours or patterns on either side.

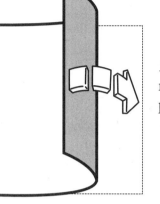

1. Start with the desired ribbon colour of the paper uppermost.

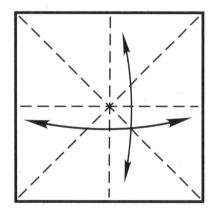

2. Precrease as shown.

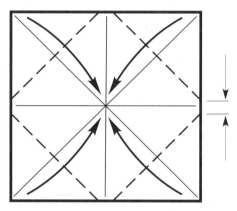

3. Fold the corners towards the centre. **Note the gap.** This gap will be the width of the ribbon.

4. Turn over.

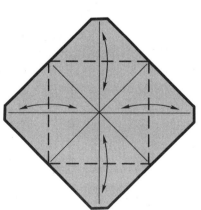

5. Fold and unfold the corners towards the centre.

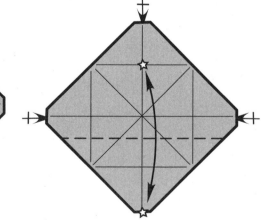

6. Fold and unfold the bottom corner up as shown, matching star to star. Then repeat for the other 3 corners.

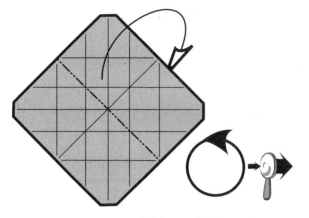

7. Mountain fold in half and rotate 45° counterclockwise. The next drawings are enlarged.

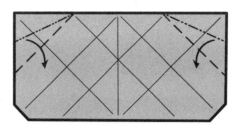

8. Squash fold the top 2 corners down towards the front.

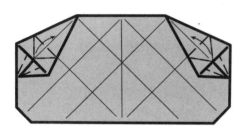

9. Petal fold the 2 sides as shown.

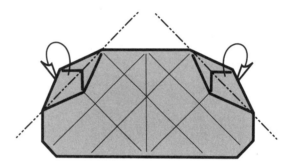

10. Mountain fold behind.

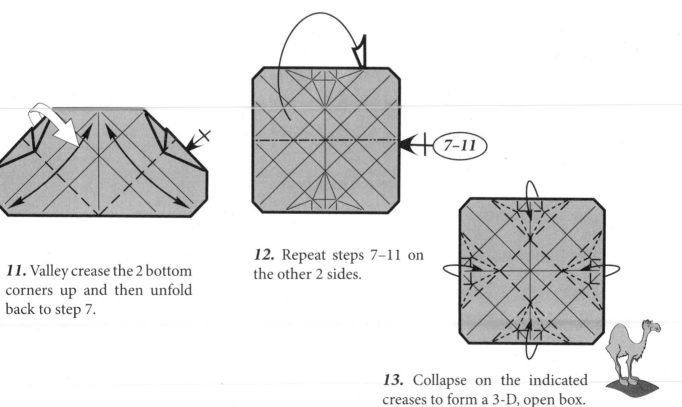

11. Valley crease the 2 bottom corners up and then unfold back to step 7.

12. Repeat steps 7–11 on the other 2 sides.

13. Collapse on the indicated creases to form a 3-D, open box.

23

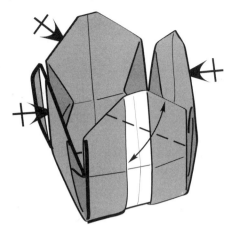

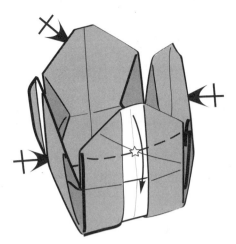

14. Precrease each flap as shown.

15. Valley fold each flap down. Note where the fold crosses the centreline, marked with a star.

16. Lift and open the right-hand side of each flap and curl it while mountain folding it in and over. Tuck the left-hand side of each flap under the curved side of the flap clockwise around the box. See the final picture.

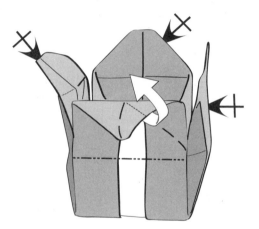

17. The finished box.

A charming one-piece box in the shape of a clam.

Choose paper with a pearlescent finish to add to the resemblance.

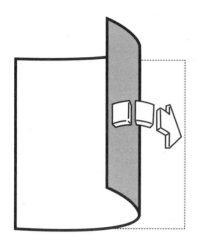

1. Begin with the white side of the paper uppermost.

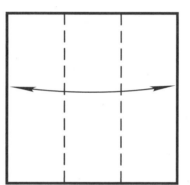

2. Divide into thirds vertically.

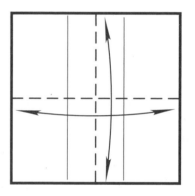

3. Valley fold in half vertically and horizontally.

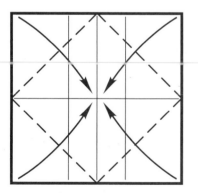

4. Blintz the corners into the middle.

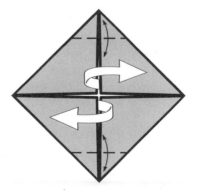

5. Valley crease the top and bottom corners and open out completely.

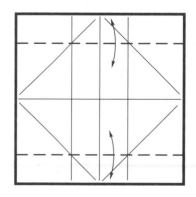

6. Valley crease across the top and bottom.

25

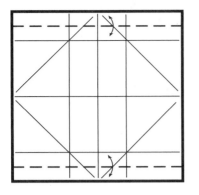

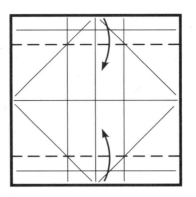

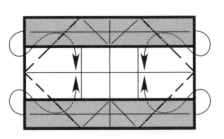

7. Valley crease as shown.

8. Valley fold down on the creases made in step 6.

9. Inside reverse fold as shown on the diagonal creases.

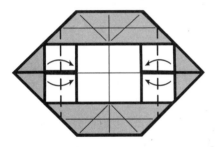

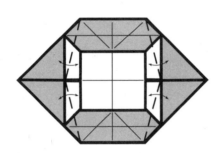

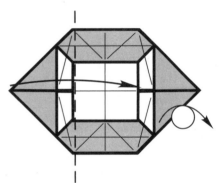

10. Valley fold the four flaps in as shown.

11. Crease diagonally on the four flaps.

12. Valley fold the left-hand point across where indicated. Turn over.

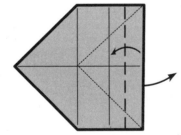

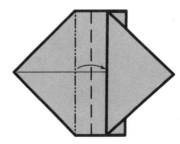

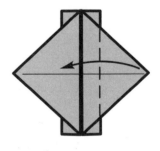

13. Valley fold the right-hand edge while allowing the flap behind to swing around to the front.

14. Crease a mountain fold on the left and then valley fold across to mirror the right-hand side.

15. Valley fold the right-hand point over.

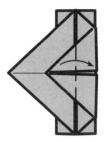

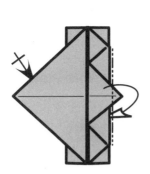

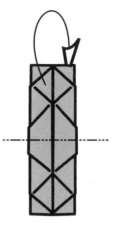

16. Valley fold the right-hand point over.

17. Mountain fold the tip behind. Repeat 15–17 on the left hand side.

18. Mountain fold in half.

19. Valley fold the front flaps out as shown. Repeat behind.

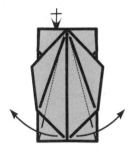

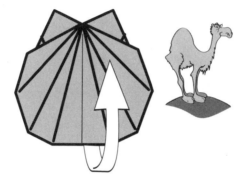

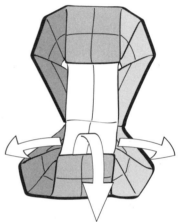

20. Swing out either side to form the basic shell shape. Repeat behind.

21. Open up the shell.

22. Carefully open out the folded over strip.

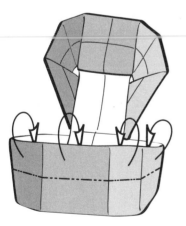

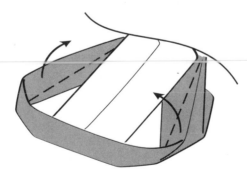

23. Using the crease, mountain fold the strip over. It will remain at 90° at the front.

24. Valley fold the sides up. Repeat 22–24 on upper half.

25. The finished box.

Snap-Lock Box

by Heinz Strobl

This is an interesting design as it can lock itself by simply pushing downwards on the top.

There is a fair amount of precreasing involved but the more accurate you are the better the end result will be.

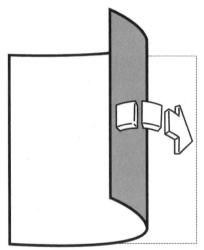

1. Lay the paper coloured side down.

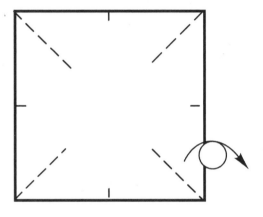

2. Pinch mark the halfway points and valley fold the diagonals as shown. Turn the paper over.

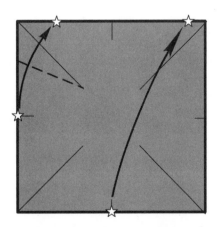

3. Line up the stars and precrease the short angle as shown. Repeat 7 times around the square.

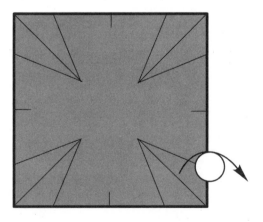

4. This is the result of step 3. Turn the paper over.

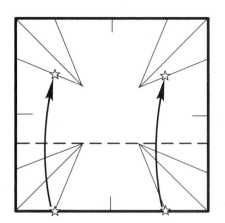

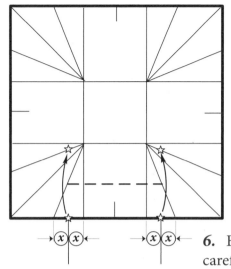

5. Line up the stars and valley fold across. Repeat 3 times around the square.

6. Examine the drawing carefully and, matching the stars, valley fold across as shown. Repeat 3 times around the square.

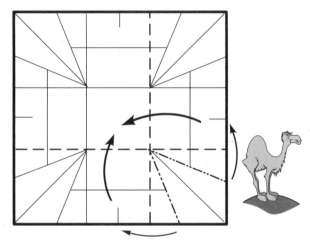

7. Pinch up one corner as shown. Paper will not lie flat.

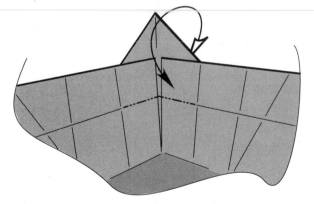

8. Mountain fold where shown to precrease the corner.

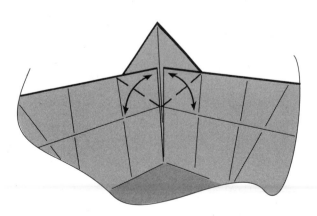

9. Valley crease the 2 flaps at the corner and repeat steps 7–9 on the other 3 corners.

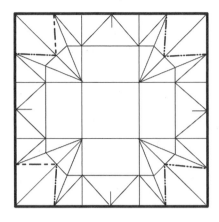

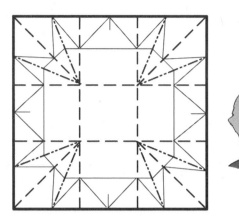

10. Mountain crease the angles at each corner. The precreasing is now complete.

11. Form the box by collapsing on the indicated creases.

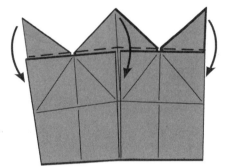

12. Fold the corners down over the outside edge to lock the form of the box.

13. To lock the box press down on the top using the previously made creases.

14. The finished box.

This delightful one-piece, closeable box is a beautiful example of simple and elegant design. If you choose rough textured paper, friction will help in keeping the box closed securely.

Pacchetto Regalo is Italian for "Gift Box".

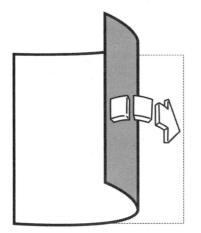

1. Start with a square, white side up.

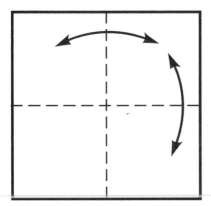

2. Crease in half both ways.

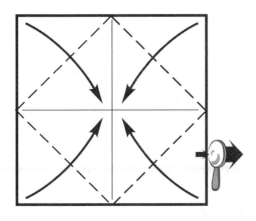

3. Blintz fold the corners.

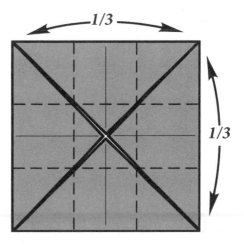

4. Crease into thirds in both directions. (See page 4).

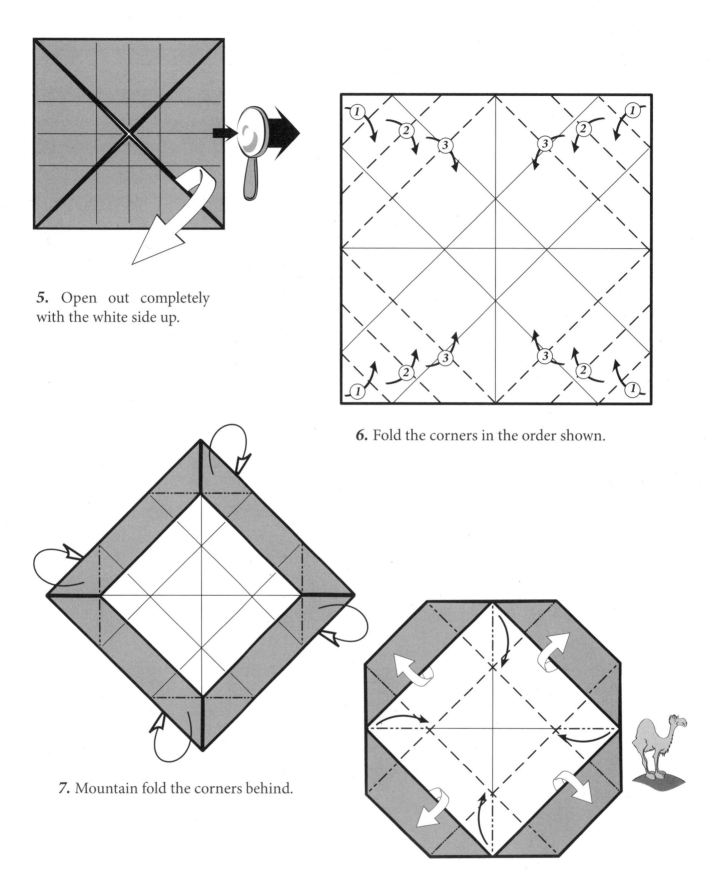

5. Open out completely with the white side up.

6. Fold the corners in the order shown.

7. Mountain fold the corners behind.

8. Using the crease shown, lift up the shaded areas and begin to form the box.

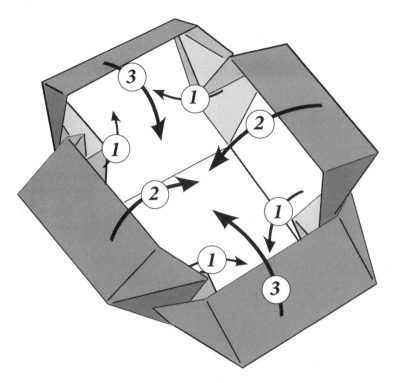

9a. Finished box version 1.

9. Examine the diagram carefully.
Fold the hinges as indicated by the arrows marked "*1*".
Bring in opposite sides, arrows marked "*2*".
And finally close with the remaining sides, arrows marked "*3*".

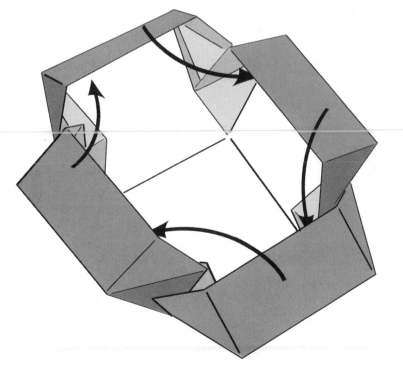

10a. Finished box version 2.

10. An alternative method of closing.

Heart Shaped Box

by Rikki Donachie

A delightfully shaped box. Perfect for enclosing a love token to one's Valentine. The precreasing enables the box to collapse beautifully into shape.

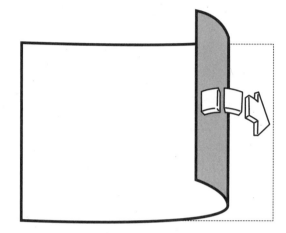

1. Begin with an "A" proportioned rectangle, coloured side down.

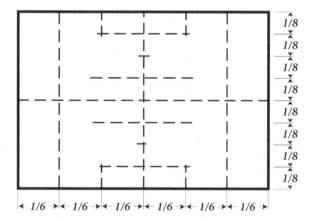

2. Start the precreasing as shown. Note: Do not make the creases longer than indicated.

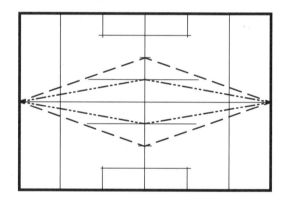

3. Continue precreasing...

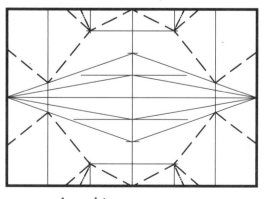

4. ...a bit more...

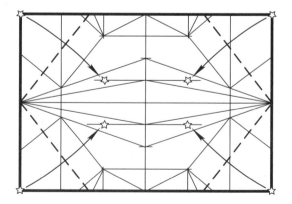

5. ...and a bit more...

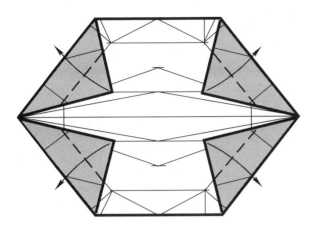

6. Fold the corners out.

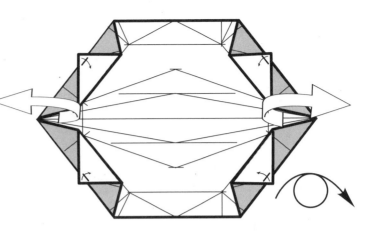

7. Fold the tips over. The pre-creasing is complete. Open out flat and turn the paper over.

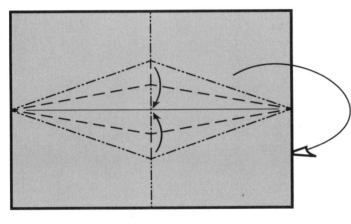

8. For clarity only the creases being used are drawn in the following steps.
Pleat the paper as shown while folding in half as indicated. Then rotate the paper.

9. Sink the top corners.

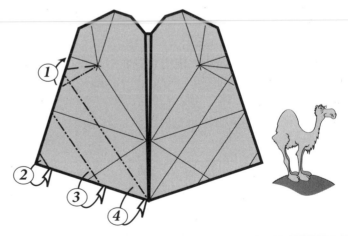

10. Using the creases, make the folds in the order shown. The paper will no longer lie flat.

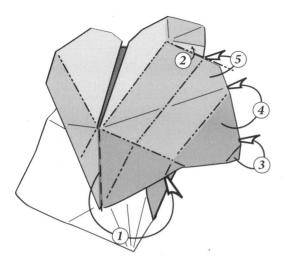

11. Reverse fold the bottom tip in (Fold 1) and repeat step 10 (Folds 2, 3, 4 and 5).

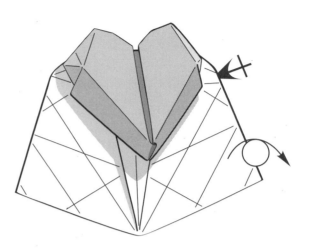

12. It should look like this. Turn the paper over and repeat 10–11 on the other side.

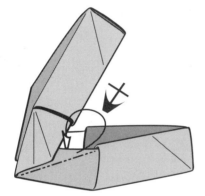

13. Mountain fold both sides in as shown.

14. The finished box.

Because the paper used is an "A" rectangle, you can make a series of boxes from A3, A4, A5, A6 and A7 which will fit one inside the other like nesting Russian dolls.

Write a message of love and put it inside the smallest box...

36

A fairly simple box which is closed with a traditional classic, the peace crane.

Box with Peace Crane
by Noriko Nagata

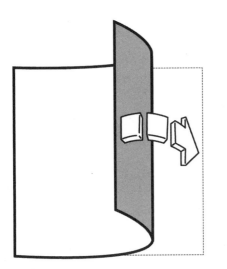

1. Begin with a square, white side up.

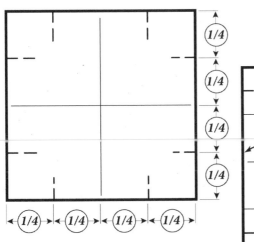

2. Crease in half horizontally and vertically and then pinch mark the quarter divisions on each side.

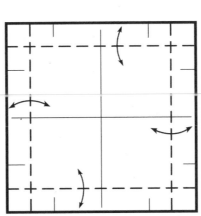

3. Precrease each side over to the quarter marks.

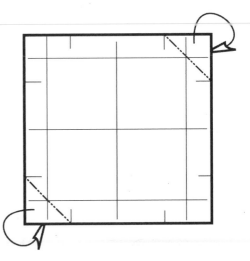

4. Mountain fold diagonally opposite corners behind as shown.

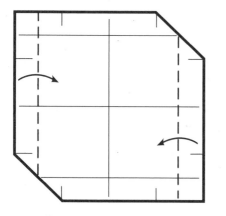

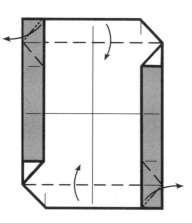

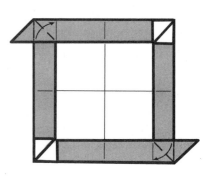

5. Valley fold the sides in on the crease.

6. Fold the top and bottom edges in while swinging the corners out.

7. Squash fold the 2 corners in.

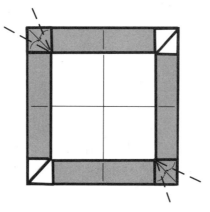

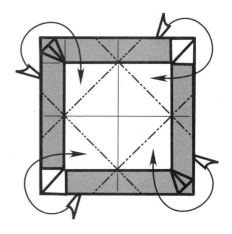

8. Valley fold the edges of each little square in, as if making a bird base.

9. Precrease diagonal mountain folds as shown.

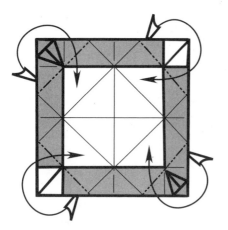

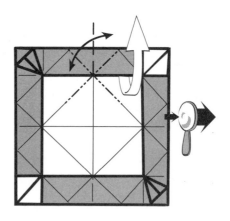

10. Mountain crease each corner behind.

11. Valley fold the short vertical as shown and open up the edge. See next picture.

38

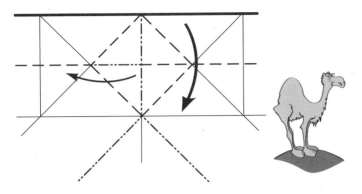

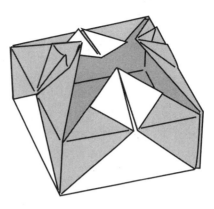

12. Look carefully at the picture and make the valley and mountain folds as shown. Collapse the edge of the paper and then repeat steps 11–12 on the other 3 sides.

13. The finished box.

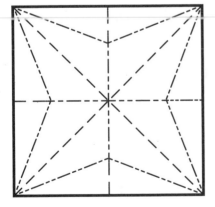

The Crane:

Take a square with sides that are half the length of the square used for the box.

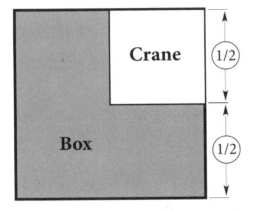

14. Fold a bird base.

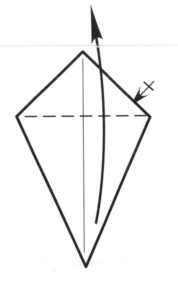

15. Valley fold the points up as far as they will go.

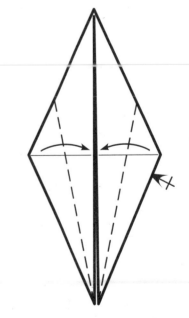

16. Valley fold the edges in to the middle, repeat behind.

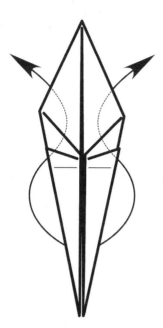

17. Inside reverse fold the points up.

18. Inside reverse fold the head.

19. Insert the little tabs on each side of the box into the pockets on each wing.

20. The finished box with a peace crane.

An unusual design of box which is extremely decorative.

It uses 7 identical squares, 3 for the base, 3 for the lid and 1 for the rose motif.

Choose fairly stiff and decorative paper that will allow for a colour change for the rose.

Triangular Box with Rose Motif

by Tomoko Fuse

Making the base:

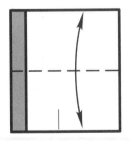

1. Lay the paper white side up.

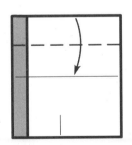

2. Pinch the halfway point and then the quarter mark as shown.

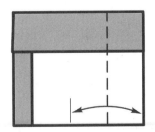

3. Valley fold the left edge to the quarter pinch mark.

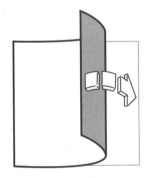

4. Crease in half horizontally.

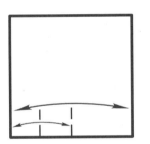

5. Fold top edge down to halfway crease.

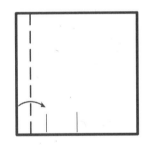

6. Valley crease right-hand edge over to central pinch mark.

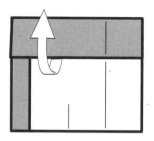

7. Open up top flap.

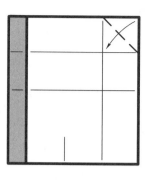

8. Valley fold top right-hand corner.

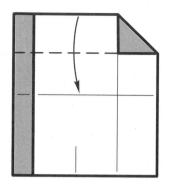

9. Refold top flap down.

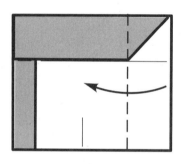

10. Valley fold right-hand edge over.

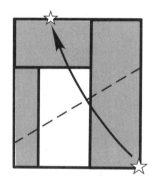

11. Valley fold right-hand corner up as shown. Match the star to the star.

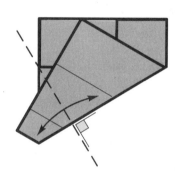

12. Crease where shown, ensuring that the crease is at 90° to the bottom edge.

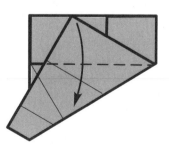

13. Fold the top flap down.

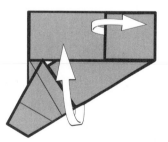

14. Partly open out the paper.

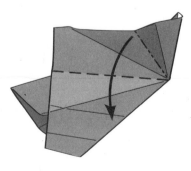

15. Make the folds as shown on the visible creases.

42

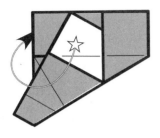 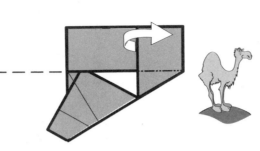 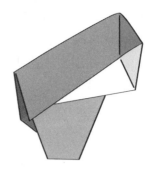

16. Tuck the white flap undeneath the flap behind it.

17. Pull out the right hand flap while bringing the lower flap up. The paper is now 3-D.

18. The complete module. Make 2 more.

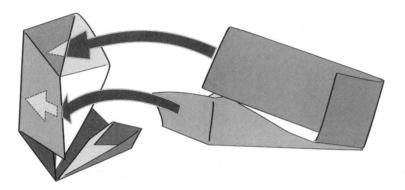

19. Tuck one module into another as shown.

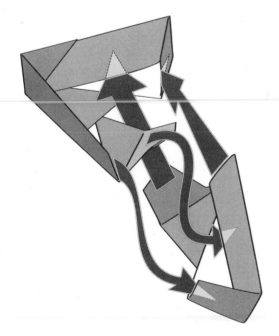 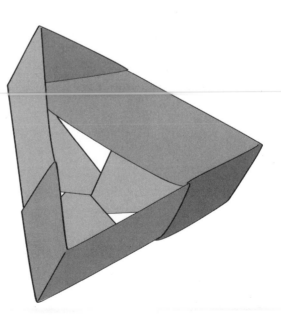

20. The third module tucks into the second and the first module tucks into the third.

21. The completed base.

Making the Lid:

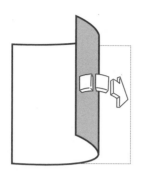

1. Lay paper white side up.

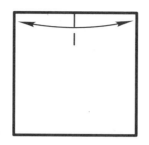

2. Pinch the halfway mark.

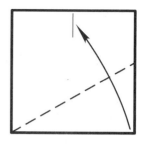

3. Fold the bottom right corner up to the halfway pinch.

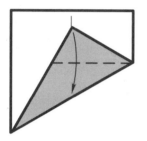

4. Valley fold the corner down.

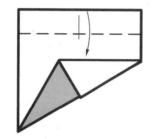

5. Valley fold the top edge down.

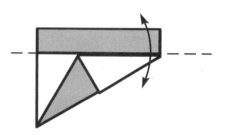

6. Valley crease where shown.

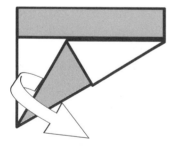

7. Partly unfold.

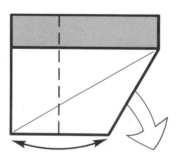

8. Valley crease where shown and unfold the flap at the rear.

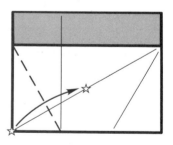

9. Valley fold the bottom left-hand corner up to the star mark on the crease.

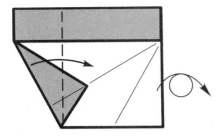

10. Fold on the crease made in step 8 and turn paper over.

11. Valley fold corner over to the left.

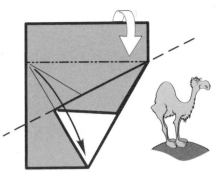

12. Bring the top rectangular section down to the sloping edge while opening up the corner behind.

13. Valley fold the little corner in.

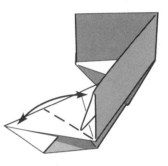

14. Valley crease the edge flap as shown. Then make 2 more identical modules.

15. Tuck the tabs of module No. 2 into the pockets of module No.1.

16. Tuck the tabs of No. 3 into the pockets of No. 2 and, at the same time the tabs of No.1 into the pockets of No. 3.
This is not easy! Be gentle and try to wriggle all of them into place a bit at a time.

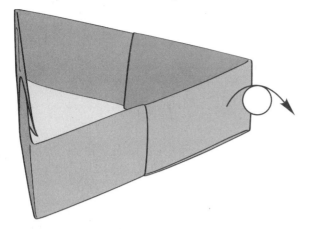

17. The completed lid, Turn over...

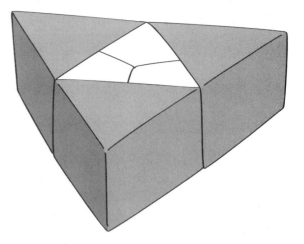

18. ...and start on the rose motif.

Making the Rose Motif:

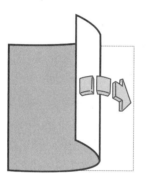

1. Lay the paper white side down.

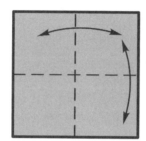

2. Crease in half vertically and horizontally.

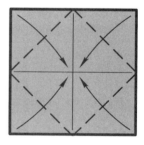

3. Fold corners to the centre.

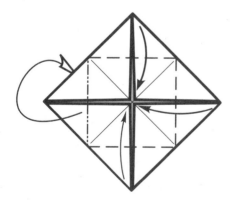

4. Mountain fold the left-hand corner behind and valley fold the other 3 corners to the front.

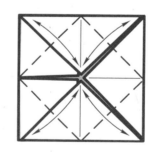

5. Valley crease all 4 corners to the centre and back.

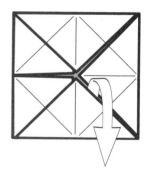

6. Open out the bottom corner downwards.

46

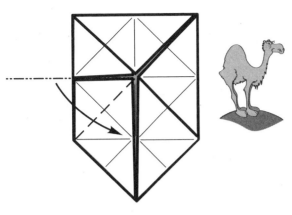

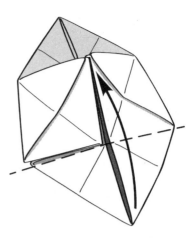

7. Bring the halfway point of the left-hand edge down and on top of the centre line. This will form a 3-D triangular pyramid.

8. Fold the lower flap up and over to touch the peak of the pyramid.

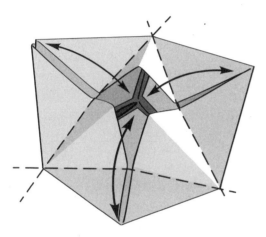

9. Valley crease across the bottom edges of the pyramid.

10. Tuck the tabs into the pockets of the lid as shown.

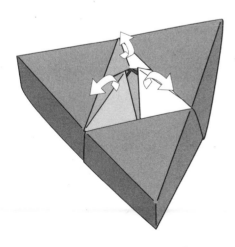

11. Peel back the 6 little flaps and curl them to form petals.

12. The finished box.

47

Pentagonal Twist Box

by Rikki Donachie

This box takes advantage of the diagonal angle of an "A" proportioned rectangle to lock the box firmly.

If a lid is not required omit step 3.

Remember! The more accurately you do the precreasing the better the end result will be.

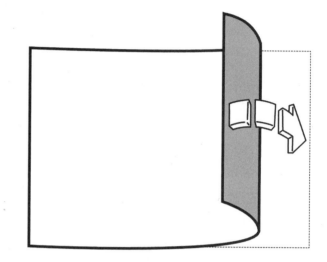

1. Start with an "A" proportioned rectangle. Lay the paper white side up.

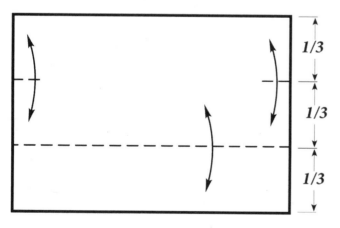

1/3

1/3

1/3

2. Precrease into thirds as shown (see page 4).

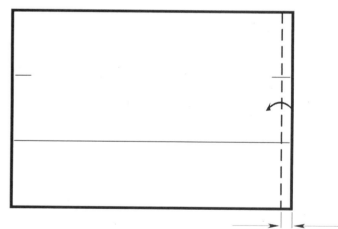

3. Valley fold the left-hand edge over by 5–8 mm.

If a lid is not required omit this step.

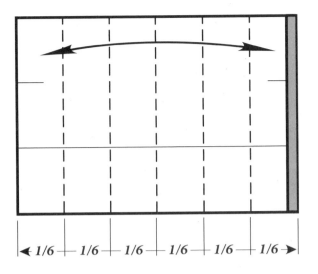

$\leftarrow$ 1/6 $\rightarrow$ 1/6 $\rightarrow$ 1/6 $\rightarrow$ 1/6 $\rightarrow$ 1/6 $\rightarrow$ 1/6 $\rightarrow$

4. Divide into sixths (Into thirds, see page 4, and then each third into half.)

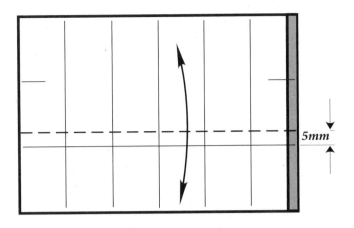

5mm

5. Valley crease where shown.

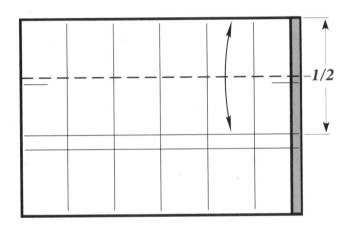

1/2

6. Valley crease halfway between the top edge and the crease made in step 5.

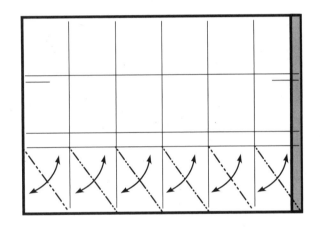

7. Mountain crease the diagonals along the bottom edge.

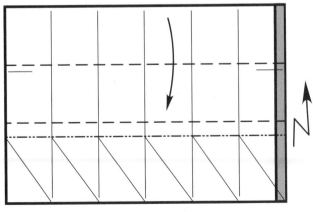

8. The precreasing is complete. Valley fold the top edge down and zig-zag fold the bottom up.

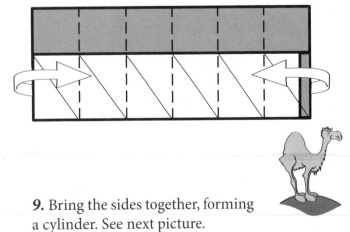

9. Bring the sides together, forming a cylinder. See next picture.

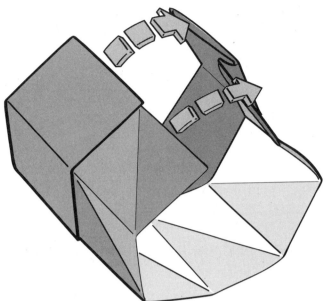

10. Form a cylinder, making sure to tuck the non-folded end inside the folded end and tighten everything up neatly.

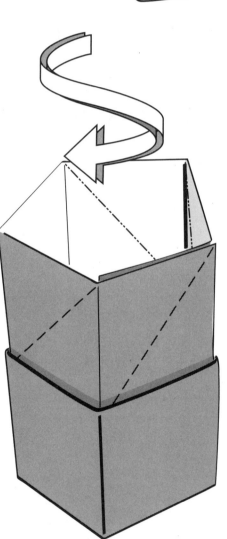

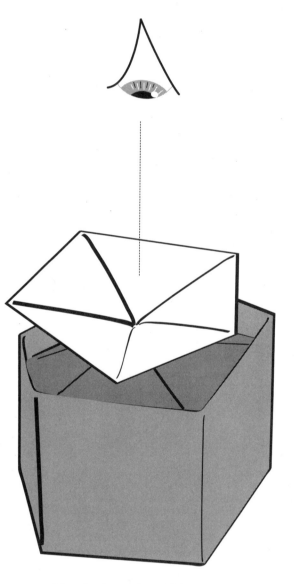

11. Using the diagonal creases, twist and press the base down. See next picture.

12. The box should look like this. The next view is looking straight down onto the base.

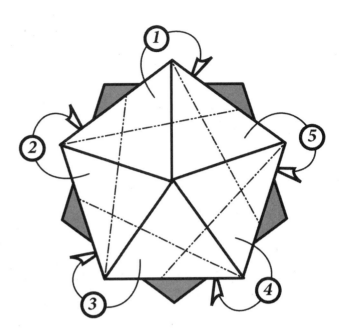

13. Mountain crease the corners behind as shown.

14. Repeat step 13 but this time in the order shown.
Note: Do not completely fold No. 1 as you will need to partially unfold it to complete No. 5.

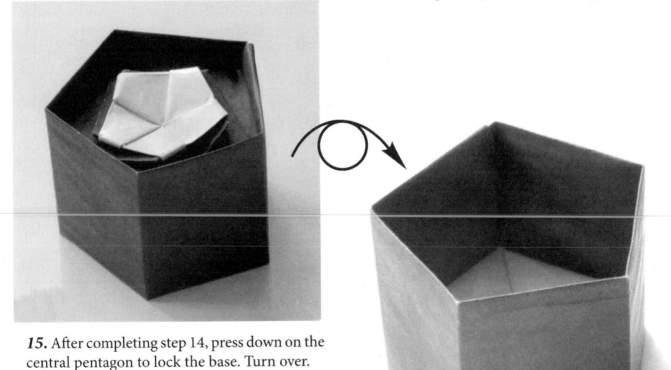

15. After completing step 14, press down on the central pentagon to lock the base. Turn over.

16. The finished box.

Twist Lid 001

The lids are made from an "A" proportioned rectangle of exactly the same size as the box.

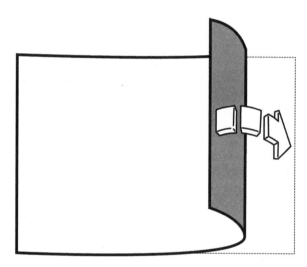

1. Lay the paper white side up.

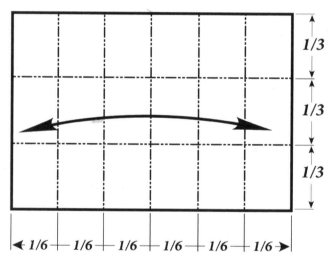

2. Precrease with mountain folds into sixths and thirds as shown. (Into thirds, see page 4, and then each third into half.)

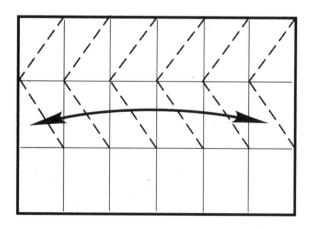

3. Precrease the diagonals with valley folds.

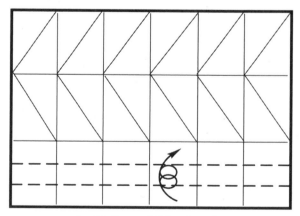

4. Valley fold the bottom edge up, over and over.

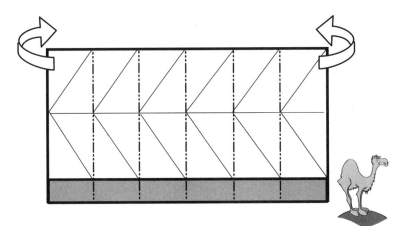

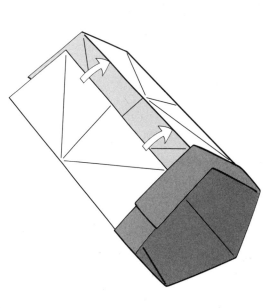

5. Bring the sides together, forming a cylinder. See next picture.

6. Make sure that the sides that overlap are fully tightened up against themselves.

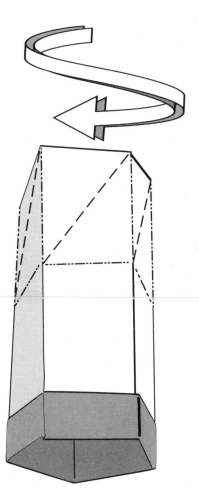

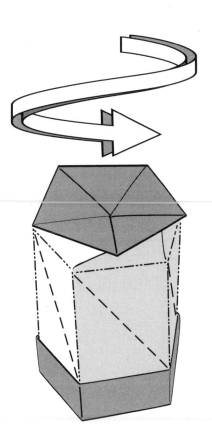

7. Push down and twist in a counterclockwise direction on the top half only. The first few times you try this you will find it awkward but, with practice, it does become easier.

8. After tidying up the top, push down and twist in a clockwise direction on the bottom half.

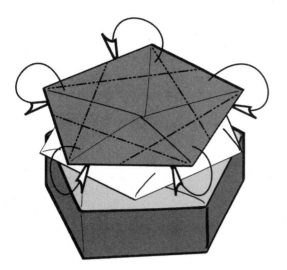

9. Mountain fold the top pentagon and lock it in the same way as steps 13 & 14 of the Twist Box, page 51.

10. The finished lid and box.

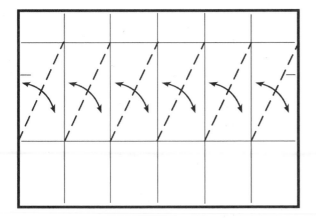

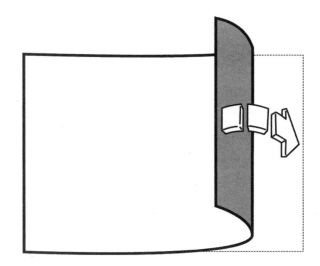

1. Lay the paper white side up.

2. Precrease with mountain folds into sixths and thirds as shown. (Into thirds, see page 4, and then each third into half.)

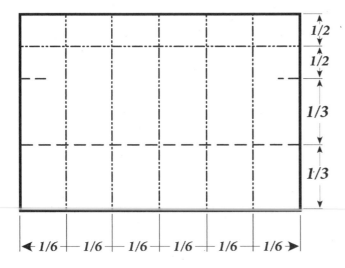

3. Precrease the diagonals with valley folds.

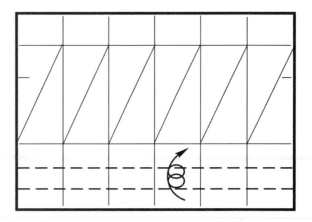

4. Valley fold the bottom edge up, over and over.

55

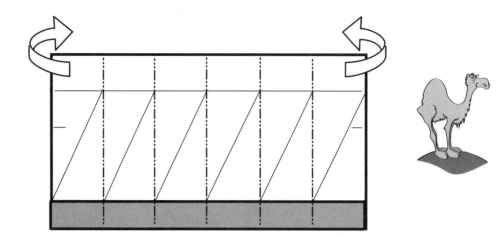

5. Bring the sides together, forming a cylinder. See next picture.

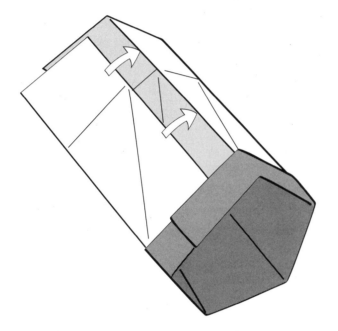

6. Make sure that the sides that overlap are fully tightened up against themselves.

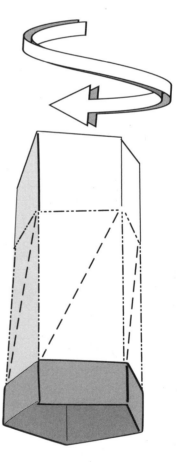

7. Twist counterclockwise on the diagonal creases and push down.

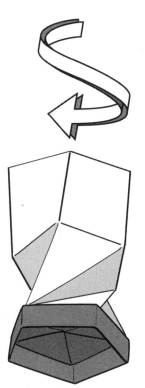

8. Continue pushing down and twisting until the top half pops down over the bottom half. Be brave! You will not rip the paper if you are careful.

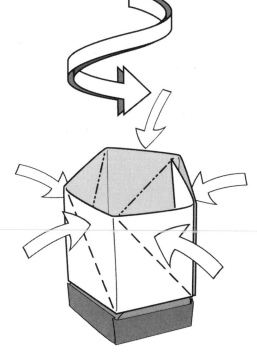

9. After tidying up the pentagonal cone formed in step 8, push in and twist the top to form a loose flower like shape. You will feel the paper "snap" into place after twisting it far enough.

10. The finished lid and box.

Twist Lid 003

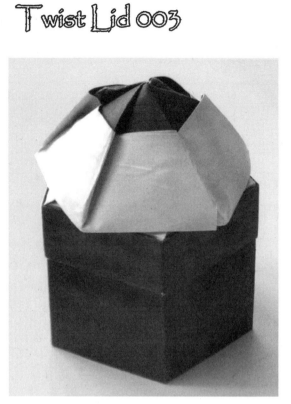

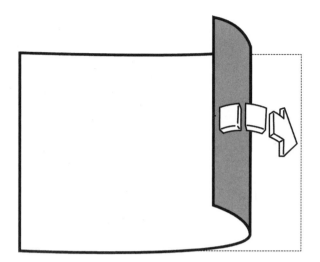

1. Lay the paper white side up.

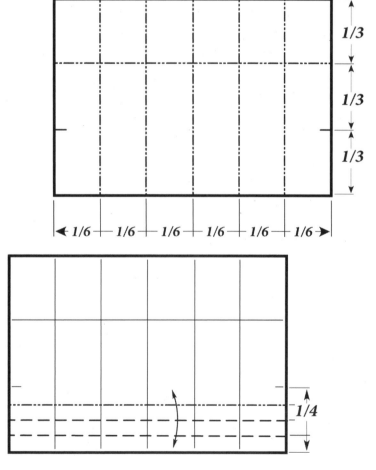

1/3

1/3

1/3

◄ 1/6 ┼ 1/6 ┼ 1/6 ┼ 1/6 ┼ 1/6 ┼ 1/6 ►

2. Precrease with mountain folds into sixths and thirds as shown. (Into thirds, see page 4, and then each third into half.)

1/4

3. Precrease the lower third into quarters.

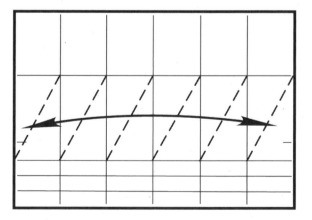

4. Precrease the diagonals with valley folds.

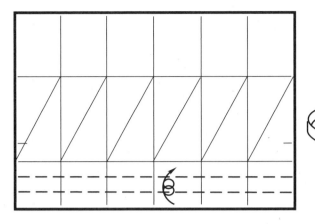

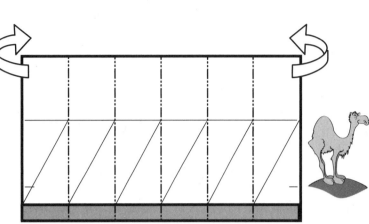

5. Valley fold the bottom edge up, over and over.

6. Bring the sides together, forming a cylinder. See next picture.

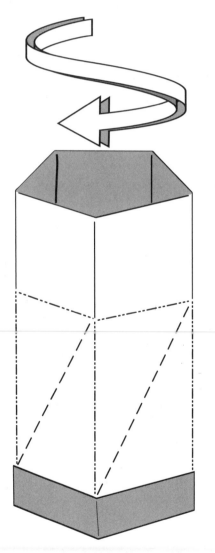

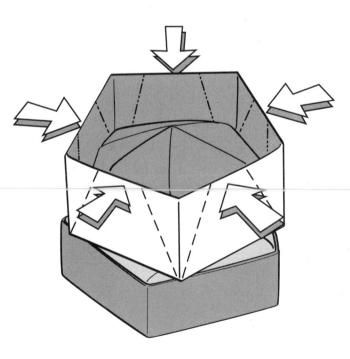

7. After tightening up and neatening the cylinder, twist and push down on the lower section to form a pentagonal cone. Then continue pushing and twisting to form a double cone. See next picture.

8. Push all 5 sides straight in to lie against the slopes of the cone, forming "ears" at each corner. Crease each ear backwards and forwards in preparation for the next step.

9. Take each ear in turn and tuck under the flaps on the inner cone. Go around at least twice to tighten up and neaten.

10. The finished box and lid.

Stretch the top two thirds of the box paper to produce a tall, thin box. The lid will remain the same.

Basic creases for a 4-sided box and lid.

Many variations of the box and lid can be achieved by altering the folds in the top two thirds (the shaded area in the drawings):

Alter the diagonals,

Bisect or trisect the small rectangles,

Stretch the proportions of the small rectangles to produce tall thin boxes.

It is also possible to alter the number of sides a box has (I have managed 3, 4, 5 & 6 sides) by dividing the main rectangle into one more section than the number of sides required. You will find that the proportions of the small rectangles will need to be changed.

I leave it to you to experiment!

Rick Beech **Editor**

Rick Beech is a professional origami expert and paper artist who lives in England with his partner Helen. He first took interest in the ancient Japanese art back in the early 70's courtesy of a children's television show presented by the legendary magician Robert Harbin, who was chosen at the time to front an entire series of "follow along at home" instructional programmes which each week demonstrated how to make something from a simple square of paper.

This discipline, using no glue or scissors, enchanted Rick from the age of 9 or 10, and he quickly developed the necessary skill whereby to fold models of infinite complexity, always hungry for new creations to make, which were not especially widespread until the popularity of the art boomed over the last 30 years. Now this challenging pastime is enjoyed as a creative pursuit by enthusiasts worldwide.

Rick's entire professional income is now drawn from origami in several ways, including the teaching of practical workshops, book authorship, to corporate entertainment, to commercial design and production of finished pieces, for advertising and marketing.

If you would like any further information or would like to book Rick to entertain you, teach you origami or accept a commission please email him at:

ricknbeech@aol.com

www.rickbeechorigami.com

Rikki Donachie **Illustrator**

Rikki was first introduced to origami as a child and took it up seriously in 1995.

He is constantly creating new and quirky designs, many of which are for commercial organisations including, the BBC, Nomura Bank, and Yellow Pages as well as countless private commisssions, others appear in publications across the world. He has been an origami consultant for BBC's *"The Apprentice"*, 2007. He has written and illustrated a book of his own original origami aeroplanes -
"Professor Dodo's Folded Paper Flying School".

He also teaches origami and pop-up card design & construction as part of the UK National Curriculum.

Apart from origami Rikki enjoys drawing, painting, pop-up card design, gardening, reading fantasy and science fiction, and learning to play the guitar.

His website can be found at:
www.itsjustabitofpaper.com   *e-mail: origamimodels@yahoo.co.uk*